The Specialty Metal Clause: Oversight Issues and Options for Congress

Valerie Bailey Grasso
Specialist in Defense Acquisition

February 6, 2014

Congressional Research Service
7-5700
www.crs.gov
RL33751

Summary

This report examines the specialty metal clause, potential oversight issues, and options for Congress. The specialty metal clause in the Defense Federal Acquisition Regulation Supplement (DFARS) prohibits the Department of Defense (DOD) from acquiring end units or components for aircraft, missile and space systems, ships, tank and automotive items, weapon systems, or ammunition unless these items have been manufactured with specialty metals that have been melted or produced in the United States. Thousands of products used for defense, aerospace, automotive, and renewable energy technologies rely on specialty metals for which there are often few, if any, substitutes. Specialty metals covered by this provision include certain types of cobalt, nickel, steel, titanium and titanium alloys, zirconium, and zirconium base alloys.

In order to preserve and protect the United States industrial base so that it could meet DOD requirements during periods of adversity and war, Congress passed a set of domestic source restrictions which became known as the Berry Amendment. In 1973, specialty metals become one of the items covered under the Berry Amendment. Over three decades later, specialty metals are now covered in a separate citation in the United States Code (U.S.C.). Congress took action in the FY2007 National Defense Authorization Act, P.L. 109-364, to separate specialty metal from the Berry Amendment (Title 10, U.S.C. 2533a).

Specialty metal provisions underwent a substantial revision in P.L. 110-181 as part of Congress's continuing effort to create a procurement environment that promotes efficiency in the DOD acquisition process, while insuring that the United States has a vigorous domestic metals industry capable of meeting defense needs. The revised specialty metal clause made clear the requirement that specific defense articles must be produced using domestic specialty metals; made exemptions for commercial-off-the-shelf (COTS) articles, electronic articles, and articles containing small amounts of non-compliant specialty metals; and allowed producers of commercially derivative defense articles to treat domestic and foreign specialty metals as fungible materials so that commercial and defense articles may be produced on the same production line without the need to trace the small amounts of metal used in each article. These changes reflected a view in Congress that there are differing rationales for offering domestic source provisions, and that these refinements would promote efficiencies throughout the defense supply chain.

In October 2013, DOD released its Annual Industrial Capabilities Report to Congress in accordance with Section 2504 of Title 10, United States Code (U.S.C.). The report states that, due to global market forces, the overall demand for rare earth materials has decreased, as prices for most rare earth oxides and metals have declined since 2011.

There are at least seven possible options for policymakers to consider: (1) eliminate the specialty metal clause; (2) require an assessment of compliance with new exceptions to the specialty metals clause; (3) require a review of waivers issued under the revised specialty metals clause, including requiring DOD to publicly disclose when waivers are granted; (4) require congressional approval before non-compliant specialty metal can be used in certain defense contracts; (5) require a congressional report for each platform/component where non-compliant specialty metals are used in defense contracts; (6) encourage the use of domestic specialty metal; and (7) appoint a special metals protection board.

Contents

Introduction 1
   Definition of Specialty Metals 1
      Exceptions to the Specialty Metals Clause 2
Major New Developments 3
   H.R. 1960/S. 1197, National Defense Authorization Act (NDAA) for Fiscal Year (FY)
      2014 3
      Subtitle B—National Defense Stockpile 3
      Directive Report Language 4
   S. 1600, Critical Minerals Policy Act of 2013 6
   H.R. 761, National Strategic and Critical Minerals Production Act of 2013 7
   H.R. 981, RARE Act of 2013 7
   H.R. 1063, National Strategic and Critical Minerals Policy Act of 2013 7
   2013 Annual Industrial Capability Report to Congress 7
   Federal Register, Final Rule on the Production of Specialty Metals 7
Background 8
   Original Congressional Intent 8
      The Test of Reasonableness 8
Oversight Issues for Congress 9
   Competition 9
      Effect on the Defense Industrial Base 9
      Competition Affects Suppliers Differently 9
      Doing Business with DOD Could Mean Maintaining Separate Production Lines 10
   Administration 11
      Administration 11
      Waivers 11
      Effect on Joint Ventures and Partnerships 12
      The Administrative Burden 13
   Reliability 13
      In Urgent Situations and Times of War 13
      Maintaining a Productive and Profitable Domestic Base 14
      Domestic Restrictions Protect the U.S. Industrial Base 14
Options for Congress 14
   Eliminate the Specialty Metal Clause 14
   Require an Assessment of Compliance with New Exceptions to the Specialty Metal
      Clause 14
   Require a Review of Waivers Issued Under the Revised Specialty Metal Clause, and
      for Public Disclosure When Waivers Are Granted 15
   Require Congressional Approval before Non-Compliant Specialty Metal Can Be
      Used In Defense Contracts 15
   Require a Congressional Report for Each Platform/Component Where Foreign
      Specialty Metals are used in Defense Contracts 16
   Encourage the Use of Domestic Specialty Metal 16
   Appoint a New Specialty Metals Protection Board 17
Legislation 17
   Legislation passed in the 112th Congress 17

FY2008 National Defense Authorization Act and Revisions to Existing Specialty
    Metal Rules 19
FY2007 National Defense Authorization Act and the Enactment of a New Specialty
    Metal Clause 20
    Section 842 of the FY2007 National Defense Authorization Act 20
Strategic Materials Protection Board 21
    2007 Meeting of the Strategic Materials Protection Board 21
    2008 Meeting of the Strategic Material Protection Board 21
Annual Industrial Capabilities Report to Congress 22
    2012 Report to Congress 23

Contacts

Author Contact Information 23

Introduction

This report examines the specialty metal clause in the Defense Federal Acquisition Regulation Supplement (DFARS), potential oversight issues, and options for Congress. The specialty metal clause prohibits DOD from acquiring end units or components for aircraft, missile and space systems, ships, tank and automotive items, weapon systems, or ammunition unless these end items or components have been manufactured with specialty metals that have been melted or produced in the United States. Specialty metals are used in components procured through DOD contracts, primarily for military aircraft, weapons, equipment, and within integrated circuits, wiring, and electrical components. Specialty metals covered by this clause include certain types of cobalt, nickel, steel, titanium and titanium alloys, zirconium, and zirconium base alloys. Thousands of products used for defense, aerospace, automotive, and renewable energy technologies rely on specialty metals for which there are often few, if any, substitutes.

The availability of sources of supply of some elements that comprise some metals, particularly the access to rare earth elements, is an issue raised in recent news reports and congressional hearings. Policymakers are interested in the specialty metal clause because the specialty metal clause affects defense contractors who produce components for commercial weapons systems.

In order to preserve and protect the United States industrial base so that it could meet DOD requirements during periods of adversity and war, in 1941 Congress passed a set of domestic source restrictions which became known as the Berry Amendment.[1] In 1973, specialty metals become one of the items covered under the Berry Amendment, a domestic preference law requiring DOD to procure items that are wholly domestic. The specialty metal clause first appeared in the 1973 Defense Appropriations Act.[2] At that time, Congress was concerned with protecting domestic source materials for the Vietnam War. At that time, the domestic specialty metal sector was hurt by subsidized imports into the United States. In order to insure an adequate domestic base for domestic items, Congress provided a guarantee to domestic suppliers for a portion of DOD's specialty metal business.

Over three decades later, specialty metals are no longer part of the Berry Amendment and are now covered in a separate citation in the United States Code (U.S.C.). Congress took action in the FY2007 National Defense Authorization Act (P.L. 109-364) to separate specialty metal from the Berry Amendment (Title 10, U.S.C. 2533a). Specialty metals are defined in 10 U.S.C. 2533b and were revised as part of the FY2008 National Defense Authorization Act (P.L. 110-181).[3]

Definition of Specialty Metals

The current definition of specialty metals can be found in 10 U.S.C. 2533b, as described here:

> Specialty Metal Defined.—In this section, the term "specialty metal" means any of the following:

---

[1] The specialty metal clause of the Berry Amendment was enacted in the 1973 DOD Appropriations Act, P.L. 92-570. For more information on the Berry Amendment, see CRS Report RL31236, *The Berry Amendment: Requiring Defense Procurement to Come from Domestic Sources*, by Valerie Bailey Grasso.

[2] P.L. 92-570, the 1973 DOD Appropriations Act, was amended to add the following text: "Wood (whether in the form of fiber or yarn or contained in fabrics, materials, or manufactured articles), or specialty metals not grown, reprocessed, reused, or produced in the United States or its possessions."

[3] The specialty metal provision of the Berry Amendment was enacted in the 1973 DOD Appropriations Act, P.L. 92-570. For more information on the Berry Amendment, see CRS Report RL31236, *The Berry Amendment: Requiring Defense Procurement to Come from Domestic Sources*, by Valerie Bailey Grasso.

(1) Steel—

(A) with a maximum alloy content exceeding one or more of the following limits: manganese, 1.65 percent; silicon, 0.60 percent; or copper, 0.60 percent; or

(B) containing more than 0.25 percent of any of the following elements: aluminum, chromium, cobalt, columbium, molybdenum, nickel, titanium, tungsten, or vanadium.

(2) Metal alloys consisting of nickel, iron-nickel, and cobalt base alloys containing a total of other alloying metals (except iron) in excess of 10 percent.

(3) Titanium and titanium alloys.

(4) Zirconium and zirconium base alloys.[4]

According to DFARS 225.252.7009,[5] specialty metals procured by DOD and used in defense articles must be melted in the United States or a "qualifying country," or melted anywhere but incorporated into an article that is manufactured in a qualifying country.[6] The specialty metals clause allows a qualifying country to manufacture parts from metal that was melted anywhere, provided it meets specifications, but a United States company can only use metal that was melted in the United States or a qualifying country.

Exceptions to the Specialty Metals Clause

The specialty metal clause provides for numerous exceptions, as described here:

- Waiver for national security purposes;
- Exceptions when compliant specialty metals are not available in satisfactory quality and sufficient quantity, in the required form, and cannot be procured as and when needed;
- Exceptions for acquisitions made outside of the United States in support of combat or contingency operations;
- Exceptions for the use of other than competitive procedures, in accordance with the Competition in Contracting Act (10 U.S.C. 2304 [c]) for circumstances of unusual and compelling urgency of need;
- Exceptions to comply with agreements with foreign governments;
- Exceptions for commissaries, exchanges, and other non-appropriated fund instrumentalities;
- Exceptions for small purchases (below the simplified acquisition threshold);
- Exceptions for electrical components;
- Exceptions for the acquisition of some commercial items;
- Exceptions for the acquisition of certain commercial-off-the-shelf items;

---

[4] For the latest DOD information on specialty metals, see Defense Logistics Agency, Information on Specialty Metals, http://www.dla.mil/J-7/metals.asp#changes.

[5] DFAR 225.252.7009 Restriction on the Acquisition of Certain Articles Containing Specialty Metals, at http://www.acq.osd.mil/dpap/dars/dfars/pdf/r20120420/252225.pdf.

[6] The qualifying countries are Austria, Belgium, Canada, Denmark, Egypt, Germany, France, Greece, Israel, Italy, Luxembourg, Netherlands, Norway, Portugal, Spain, Sweden, Switzerland, Turkey, United Kingdom and Northern Ireland. See DFAR 225.252.7014.

- Exceptions for the acquisition of components if there is less than 2% of noncompliant metal (called the "de minimis" exception);
- Exceptions for the acquisition of certain commercially derivative defense articles[7]; and
- Exceptions for the acquisition of certain noncompliant materials if the Secretary of Defense certifies in writing that acceptance of such materials is required for reasons of national security, including certain conditions and requirements.[8]

Major New Developments

H.R. 1960/S. 1197, National Defense Authorization Act (NDAA) for Fiscal Year (FY) 2014

H.R. 1960 was introduced in the House on May 14, passed the House in a recorded vote (315-108) on June 14, and was referred to the Senate on July 8, 2013.[9] S. 1197 was introduced on June 20, 2013 and referred to the Armed Services Committee. The bill contains several provisions which give the President more authority to conserve strategic and critical materials, as well as direct the Secretary of Defense to report on plans to assess the supply chain diversification for rare earth substitutes and develop risk mitigation strategies. The provisions appear below.

Subtitle B—National Defense Stockpile

Section 1411. Use of National Defense Stockpile for the Conservation of a Strategic and Critical Materials Supply

Section 1411 modifies the President's authority to maintain and manage a national defense stockpile, and allow the Defense Logistics Agency to more proactively engage in the market. These changes would grant the President the authority to conserve strategic and critical materials.

(a) Presidential Responsibility for Conservation of Stockpile Materials - Section 98e (a) of Title 50, United States Code, is amended:

(1) by redesignating paragraphs (5) and (6) as paragraphs (6) and (7), respectively; and

(2) by inserting after paragraph (4) the following new paragraph (5):

"(5) provide for the recovery of any strategic and critical material from excess materials made available for recovery purposes by other Federal agencies;"

(b) Uses of National Defense Stockpile Transaction Fund - Section 98h (b) (2) of Title 50, United States Code, is amended—

---

[7] This exception allows producers of commercial derivative defense articles, like fasteners, to treat domestic and foreign specialty metals as fungible, so that commercial and defense articles may be produced on the same production line without the need to trace the source of the metal used in each article.

[8] Title 10, Subtitle A, Part IV, Chapter 148, Subchapter V, 2533b. Requirement to buy strategic materials critical to national security from American sources; exceptions; http://www.acq.osd mil/dpap/cpic/ic/restrictions_on_specialty_metals_10_usc_2533b.html.

[9] Public Law (P.L.) 113-66 was signed into law on December 26, 2013.

(1) by redesignating subparagraphs (D) through (L) as subparagraphs (E) through (M), respectively; and

(2) by inserting after subparagraph (C) the following new subparagraph (D): "(D) Encouraging the conservation of strategic and critical materials."

(c) Development of Domestic Sources - Section 98h-6(a) of Title 50, United States Code, is amended, in the matter preceding paragraph (1), by inserting 'and conservation' after 'development'.

Section 1412. Authority to Acquire Additional Materials for the National Defense Stockpile

Section 1412 provides authority to acquire certain additional strategic and critical materials for the National Defense Stockpile. The materials anticipated to be acquired have been identified to meet the military, industrial, and essential civilian needs of the United States.

(a) Acquisition Authority - Using funds available in the National Defense Stockpile Transaction Fund, the National Defense Stockpile Manager may acquire the following materials determined to be strategic and critical materials required to meet the defense, industrial, and essential civilian needs of the United States:

(1) Ferroniobium.

(2) Dysprosium Metal.

(3) Yttrium Oxide.

(4) Cadmium Zinc Tellurium Substrate Materials.

(5) Lithium Ion Precursors.

(6) Triamino-Trinitrobenzene and Insensitive High Explosive Molding Powders.

(b) Amount of Authority - the National Defense Stockpile Manager may use up to $41,000,000 of the National Stockpile Transaction Fund for acquisition of the materials specified in subsection (a).

(c) Fiscal Year Limitation - The authority under this section is available for purchases during Fiscal Year 2014 through Fiscal Year 2019.

Directive Report Language

In H.R. 1960, under Title XVI, Industrial Base Matters, there are two reporting requirements required by the House Armed Services Committee that address congressional concerns over maintaining a secure access and a diverse supply chain for rare earth elements to be used for national security purposes and in defense weapon systems.

The first directive requires the Under Secretary of Defense for Acquisition, Technology and Logistics to submit a report to the congressional defense committees, by February 1, 2014, to outline a risk mitigation strategy focused on securing the necessary supplies of rare earth elements. The report language reads as follows:

Title XVI – Industrial Base Matters

Report on the Diversification of Supply Activities Related to Rare Earth Elements

The committee is aware that in response to the report required by section 843 of the Ike Skelton National Defense Authorization Act for Fiscal Year 2011 (P.L. 111-383) and based on forecasting demand for fiscal year 2013 only, the Under Secretary of Defense for Acquisition, Technology, and Logistics concluded that domestic production of rare earth elements could satisfy the level of consumption required to meet defense procurement needs by fiscal year 2013, with the exception of yttrium. However, the committee observes that the Future Years Defense Program indicates that consumption of rare earth elements is expected to increase after 2013. Specifically, the report on the feasibility and desirability of recycling, recovery, and reprocessing of rare earth elements required by the conference report (H.Rept. 112-329) to accompany the National Defense Authorization Act for Fiscal Year 2012, states that each SSN-774 *Virginia*-class submarine would require approximately 9,200 pounds of rare earth materials, each DDG-51 Aegis destroyer would require approximately 5,200 pounds of these materials, and each F-35 Lightning II aircraft would require approximately 920 pounds of these materials.

The committee is aware that the Department of Defense intends to pursue a three-pronged strategy to secure supplies of rare earth elements, which consists of diversification of supply, pursuit of substitutes, and a focus on reclamation of waste, as part of a larger U.S. Government recycling effort. The committee believes that diversification of supply activities related to rare earth elements is necessary in order to meet the growing demand for these materials, but the committee is concerned that some of these processes may prove to be technically difficult or so expensive that they are deemed cost-prohibitive.

Therefore, the committee directs the Under Secretary of Defense for Acquisition, Technology, and Logistics to submit a report to the congressional defense committees by February 1, 2014, on the Department's risk mitigation strategy for rare earth elements, which should include, at a minimum, the following elements:

(1) A list and description of the programs initiated or planned to reclaim rare earth elements by the Department, along with a description of the materials reclaimed or expected to be reclaimed from such programs;

(2) An assessment of the cost of materials produced by these reclamation efforts compared to the cost of newly-mined materials;

(3) An assessment of availability of reliable suppliers in the National Defense Industrial Base for the reclamation and reprocessing of rare earth elements;

(4) A list of alternative sources of supply, such as mine tailings, recycled components, and consumer waste, that the Department has investigated or plans to investigate;

(5) A physical description of alternative sources of supply with corresponding geologic characteristics, such as grade, resource size, and the amenability of that feedstock to metallurgical processing;

(6) A description of the materials that the Department plans to obtain via the Defense Priorities and Allocations System; and

(7) Other diversification of supply activities deemed relevant by the Under Secretary.[10]

The second directive requires DOD to perform an assessment of the potential for incorporating the substitution of non-rare earth materials into components of the Joint Strike Fighter, based on the supply chain challenges faced in securing components containing rare earth materials.

Report on the Implementation of Rare Earth Elements Strategy in the Joint Strike Fighter Program

The committee is aware that the Department of Defense intends to pursue a three-pronged strategy to secure supplies of rare earth elements, which consists of diversification of supply, pursuit of substitutes, and a focus on reclamation of waste as part of a larger U.S. Government recycling effort. However, it remains unclear how this strategy will be implemented in the Department's major defense acquisition programs (MDAPs). Several high-profile MDAPs, including the F-35 Lightening II program, may use significant amounts of rare earth elements in full-rate production. The committee is concerned that the introduction of substitute materials and components may increase acquisition and sustainment costs through the qualification of manufacturers for substitutes, implementation of engineering changes to accommodate substitutes, and the long-term costs associated with supplier networks.

Therefore, the committee directs the Assistant Secretary of the Navy for Research, Development and Acquisition, in coordination with the Program Executive Officer for the F-35, to submit a report to the congressional defense committees by February 15, 2014, on the potential for substitution of components and materials into F-35 aircraft to reduce consumption of rare earth materials. The report, which may include a classified annex, should include the following:

(1) A list and description of subsystems that contain rare earth elements and the approximate quantities of each rare earth element by subsystem;

(2) An assessment of the potential to incorporate substitute components or materials in each subsystem based on technical acceptability, to include consideration of performance requirements, and engineering changes that may be necessary for integration of the substitute; and

(3) An assessment of the potential to incorporate substitute components or materials in each subsystem based on cost acceptability to include consideration of material costs, qualification and testing costs, and engineering change costs.[11]

S. 1600, Critical Minerals Policy Act of 2013

S. 1600, the Critical Minerals Policy Act of 2013, was introduced on October 29, 2013, and referred to the Energy and Natural Resources Committee. The bill would require the Secretary of Interior and the Secretary of Energy to amend current policies, including "facilitate the reestablishment of domestic, critical mineral designation, assessment, production, manufacturing, recycling, analysis, forecasting, workforce, education, research, and international capabilities in the United States."[12] The Senate Energy and Natural Resources Committee held a hearing on the bill on January 28, 2014. The bill has 18 sponsors and bi-partisan support.

---

[10] H.Rept. 113-102, to accompany H.R. 1960, the proposed National Defense Authorization Act for Fiscal Year 2014.
[11] H.Rept. 113-102, to accompany H.R. 1960, the proposed National Defense Authorization Act for Fiscal Year 2014.
[12] S. 1600, the Critical Minerals Policy Act of 2013.

H.R. 761, National Strategic and Critical Minerals Production Act of 2013

H.R. 761, the National Strategic and Critical Minerals Production Act of 2013 was introduced on February 15, 2013, and referred to the Committee on Natural Resources on July 8, 2013, (H.Rept. 113-138). The bill passed in a recorded vote, 246-178, and was referred to the Senate Energy and Natural Resources Committee on December 19, 2013. The bill would require both the Secretary of the Interior and the Secretary of Agriculture to more efficiently develop domestic sources of the minerals and materials of strategic and critical importance to U.S. economic and national security, and manufacturing competitiveness.[13]

H.R. 981, RARE Act of 2013

H.R. 981, the RARE Act of 2013, was introduced on March 6, 2013, referred to the Subcommittee on Energy and Mineral Resources on March 7, 2013, and ordered to be reported by Unanimous Consent on May 15, 2013. The bill would require the Secretary of Interior to conduct an assessment of current global rare earth element resources and the potential future global supply.

H.R. 1063, National Strategic and Critical Minerals Policy Act of 2013

H.R. 1063, the National Strategic and Critical Minerals Policy Act of 2013, was introduced on March 12, 2013, referred to the Subcommittee on Energy and Mineral Resources on March 15, 2013, and ordered to be reported by unanimous consent on May 15, 2013. The bill would require the Secretary of the Interior to conduct an assessment of the current and future demands for the minerals critical to United States manufacturing, agricultural competitiveness, economic and national security.

2013 Annual Industrial Capability Report to Congress

The 2013 Annual Industrial Capability Report to Congress can be accessed online, at http://www.acq.osd.mil/mibp/docs/annual_ind_cap_rpt_to_congress-2013.pdf.

Federal Register, Final Rule on the Production of Specialty Metals

DOD has sought public comment regarding the definition of the word "produced" regarding the production of specialty metals. P.L. 111-383 required DOD to seek public comment regarding the application of the word "produce" as applied to the production of specialty metals. On July 24, 2012, DOD published a proposed rule to amend the DFARS to revise the definition of the word "produce." In the proposed revision and in response to public comments, DOD is proposing to remove certain processes—"quenching and tempering"—from armor plate production, and to "expand the application of the other listed technologies, currently restricted just to titanium and titanium alloys, to any special metal that could be formed by such technologies." The public

---

[13] H.R. 4402, the National Strategic and Critical Minerals Production Act of 2012 was introduced on July 16, 2012, and referred to the Committee on Energy and Natural Resources.

comment period ended on September 24, 2012, and the final rule was issued on March 28, 2013.[14]

Background

Original Congressional Intent

Beginning with the 1973 Defense Appropriations Act, some Members of Congress advocated for a thoughtful and reasonable approach in adding specialty metal to the list of items covered under the Berry Amendment. In the ensuing debate over specialty metal, Senator Jacob Javits discussed the intent of the legislation:

> As an example, I would certainly hope that the Department of Defense in administering this provision would take into consideration the fact that it would be a virtual impossibility for a company participating in a defense contract to try to ascertain for itself, let alone for the myriad of suppliers of small component metals parts, that there was no small amount of metals used which would come within the definition of specialty metals. I would hope that the Department of Defense in the administration of this provision, while seeking to carry out the broad intent of protecting the special metals industry, would have sufficient flexibility and discretion under this provision so that they would not be required to go to ridiculous extremes which would result in an almost impossible administrative burden placed upon Government contractors, and the addition of needless expenses to the Government in carrying out its procurement practices.[15]

The Test of Reasonableness

From the inception of the specialty metal clause, both Congress and DOD emphasized that a test of reasonableness would be applied so that the specialty metal clause would not pose an administrative burden upon DOD contractors or the federal government.

In a March 7, 2007, hearing before the House Armed Services Committee, Air and Land Forces Subcommittee, Lieutenant General Donald J. Hoffman, Air Force military deputy, asked that Congress give its support to relieving the Air Force from the more arduous aspects of the specialty metal waiver process, as discussed below:

> I would ask for the Committee's continued help in one area, and that is the area of specialty metals. In last year's authorization act, Congress provided some relief in the area of electronic components, where the source of minute amounts of specialty metals cannot be traced throughout the commercial production supply chain. This relief is certainly helpful, but I would ask that there be further consideration for relief in the area of commercial products. Tracing the source of metals and commercial products is very problematic for industry, particularly where DOD is a very small part of their market. The cost of creating a separate supply chain that is able to trace specialty metals down to the lowest tier, such as fasteners, is something industry has been unwilling to accept if it is to remain commercially competitive.

> While the Congress has authorized a waiver process, the justification and support of the waivers can be very labor intensive. As an example, the waiver process last year for the

---

[14] DFARS Case 2012-D041. Specialty Metals and the Definition of "Produce." *Federal Register*, Vol. 78, No. 60, March 28, 2013, at http://www.acq.osd mil/dpap/dars/dfars/changenotice/2013/20130328/fr_2012-D041.pdf.

[15] Excerpt from Senator Jacob Javits' remarks on the passage of H.R. 16593, Making Appropriations for the Defense Establishment for Fiscal Year 1973. 118 Congressional Record S17967 (October 13, 1972).

AMRAM (Advanced Medium Range Air-to-Air) missile, the government contractor spent over 2,200 man hours to review 4,000 parts, and produced a documentation to justify the waiver. This documentation was eight inches tall in printed form. All this work was to justify a waiver for $14,000 on an item that is valued at $566,000.[16]

Oversight Issues for Congress

The specialty metal clause prohibits DOD from procuring metal that is not produced in the United States.[17] Three issues stand out as policy questions that Congress may choose to consider in its oversight role. First, how does the specialty metal clause affect competition among the different contractor tiers in the U.S. defense industrial base? Second, what are the factors that contribute to the success or failure of the administration of the specialty metal clause? Third, how does one weigh the reliability of having a domestic supplier base in times of urgent and compelling need, coupled with the desire to promote global trade?

Congress may want to consider whether recent revisions in the specialty metal clause have adequately addressed the purpose of the law, as well as concerns raised about how the new rules are implemented.

Competition

Effect on the Defense Industrial Base

Competition for defense work is affected by the availability of sufficient quantity and quality of specialty metal; such metal may be critical and vital to the war-fighting effort if it is used for "high-tech" electronics and communications like personal digital assistants. Creating separate electronic chips for military use only, with no foreign content, would be an expensive undertaking, and some companies have elected not to do so even if it means not being able to sell to DOD.

Congress addressed this issue by exempting electronic components from the specialty metals clause.

> ... unless the Secretary of Defense, upon the recommendation of the Strategic Materials Protection Board pursuant to 10 U.S.C. 187, determines that the domestic availability of a particular electronic component is critical to national security.[18]

Competition Affects Suppliers Differently

Some defense suppliers have framed the specialty metals debate as one between companies that advocate for global trade versus those that favor a dedicated domestic industrial supplier base. On the one hand, some argue that major aerospace companies are eager to seek waivers of domestic source restrictions because doing so would increase their access to foreign markets for specialty metal. Some industry leaders have maintained a view that domestic source restrictions like the

---

[16] Statement of Lieutenant General Donald J. Hoffman, Military Deputy, Office of the Assistant Secretary of the Air Force for Acquisition, before the Subcommittee of Air and Land Forces, House Armed Services Committee, March 7, 2007.

[17] 10 U.S.C. §2533a, Requirement to Buy Certain Articles from American Sources; Exceptions.

[18] 252.225.70-Authorization Acts, Appropriations Acts, and Other Statutory Restrictions on Foreign Acquisition (Revised March 17, 2011), at http://www.acq.osd mil/dpap/dars/dfars/html/current/225_70 htm#225.7003-3.

Berry Amendment are inconsistent with a policy to encourage global competition. Yet some others believe that the presence of competition, particularly from the foreign markets, makes it more difficult for domestic suppliers to survive. Each supplier in the defense industrial base views competition differently.

For example, some major defense contractors have contended that global competition for commercial and defense work requires establishing and developing foreign trading partners, and that the capacity of domestic suppliers to meet the needs of major defense contractors is insufficient. Some contractors, especially those whose primary market is the U.S. defense industry, know their client base and what they have to buy, and thus are locked into one dedicated supply chain. Yet many other contractors, particularly at the third and fourth tiers of the supply chain, market to both military and commercial sectors; they find that carrying separate supply chains is cost-prohibitive and poses a significant administrative burden. Some companies may not know who the ultimate purchaser of their product will be, so they cannot be certain whether the end use is for a commercial or military application.

The specialty metals clause addresses these concerns: (1) specialty metal from many allied countries is already exempt from the domestic source requirement because of the existence of Memoranda of Understanding (MOU) with the United States, which guarantee that allied suppliers be given equal treatment in DOD procurement;[19] (2) commercial-off-the-shelf (COTS) items are exempt from the specialty metal clause so that suppliers who sell identical commercial and defense articles are exempt from the specialty metal clause; (3) recent changes to the special metals clause allow producers of commercial derivative defense articles and fasteners to treat domestic and foreign specialty metals as fungible materials so that commercial and defense items may be produced on the same production line without the need to trace the source of the metal used in each item.

Congress may want to consider whether recent revisions in the specialty metal clause have adequately addressed this issue, and identify and monitor the impact of this provision within DOD and the DOD supply chain.

Doing Business with DOD Could Mean Maintaining Separate Production Lines

The specialty metal clause as contained in the Berry Amendment required 100% compliance; there was no clause for non-compliant metal. As an example, when DOD purchased avionics, electronics, components, and subassemblies, items with specialty metal were required to be 100% domestic. However, the integration of the global supply chain meant that cheaper, foreign metal could make up virtually all products, and that there were fewer companies that could certify that all of the metal used in the production of their items was wholly domestic in origin. Suppliers who wanted to sell to DOD and to the commercial sector could be forced to maintain two separate production lines; this would raise DOD's costs.

Congress addressed this issue by exempting electronic components from the specialty metal clause, exempting any article containing "de minimis" amounts of specialty metals that were not melted in the United States (de minimis is defined as when non-compliant specialty metal is less than 2% of the total weight of specialty metals in the item). As mentioned earlier, producers of

---

[19] See list of qualifying countries at http://www.acq.osd mil/dpap/dars/dfars/html/current/252225 htm#252.225-7012. These countries are allies of the United States. Japan is an ally and significant specialty metal producing country but is not listed here, largely attributed to the fact that Japan has a constitutional prohibition on weapons production.

commercial derivative defense items like fasteners can treat domestic and foreign specialty metals as fungible materials so that commercial and defense items may be produced on the same production line without the need to trace the source of the metal used in each item.

Administration

Administration

Can DOD administer and properly execute the new specialty metal clause? The new specialty metal clause may not be entirely enforceable, because it may be nearly impossible to determine to any degree of certainty whether the smallest of the nuts, bolts, screws, and fasteners that make up DOD weapons systems and equipment are of 100% domestic content. Given the recent revisions in the exceptions for electronic components, COTS items, and items with de minimis amounts of non-compliant metal, and the fungible use of specialty metals in commercial derivative articles, items, and fasteners, it may prove difficult for Congress to assess how effectively the specialty metals clause can be administered. Such an assessment would in all likelihood require that DOD collect data on the use of specialty metals under the new rules.

Waivers

The debate over the specialty metal clause was largely fueled by voluntary disclosures, made by companies who sell to DOD, which the companies were in violation of the Berry Amendment specialty metal requirement. For example, the National Semiconductor Corporation disclosed that specialty metal used in its products did not meet the requirement. "To the best of our knowledge, no other semiconductor manufacturer currently is capable of meeting that standard," then wrote Gerry Fields, vice president; Texas Instruments and the Intel Corporation made similar disclosures. Each company stated that, due to the global supply chain for its production line, it would be unable to meet present and future specialty metal requirements.[20] The Semiconductor Industry Association (SIA), which represents about 85% of U.S.-based semiconductor industry, stated that integrated circuits from products made by SIA member companies may contain small quantities of non-compliant specialty metal. Such quantities constitute a small percentage of the item's overall metal content. Further, SIA opined that the application of a domestic preference to specialty metal, as currently applied by DOD and the FY2007 Defense Authorization bill, did not take into account the economic realities that have shaped the development of the specialty metal industry and indeed the entire global technology sector.[21]

---

[20] Memorandum on Berry Amendment/Buy American Act - DFARS Clause 252.225-7014, Gerry Fields, Vice-President, Worldwide Quality Network and New Product Execution. National Semiconductor Corporation, March 7, 2006; also, Request for Confirmation of Compliance with the Berry Amendment, by Brent Thornton, Quality Assurance Manager, Hirel, Defense, and Aerospace Products, March 23, 2006; Memorandum on Domestic Preference for Specialty Metals, *Texas Instruments*, May 12, 2006.

[21] SIA's Position on the Berry Amendment, May 9, 2006. Since 1977, SIA has identified itself as a leading voice for the semiconductor industry. SIA member companies comprise more than 85% of the U.S. semiconductor industry. Collectively, the chip industry employs a domestic workforce of 225,000 people. According to SIA, over 70% of U.S. manufacturing facilities are on U.S. soil, but greater than 75% of the industry revenue is affected by specialty metal provisions. These provisions affect military contracts and the availability of commercial products for the military. SIA points out that procurement regulation affect semiconductors in two ways: first, the military relies on a commercial off-the-shelf (COTS) acquisition model for many components. Second, semiconductors are used in downstream products supplied under military contracts and subcontracts. Because of these trends, they note their customers have a more direct exposure to government procurement than do semiconductor companies themselves; see http://www.sia-online.org.

During FY2007, DOD approved a "Domestic Non-Availability Determination (DNAD)" to permit the procurement of non-compliant (non-domestic) fasteners.[22] As several suppliers voluntarily disclosed their use of non-compliant specialty metal in defense weapon systems, DOD proposed a temporary modification to the specialty metal clause through a series of interim instructions. On March 10, 2006, the Defense Contract Management Agency issued guidance to its contracting officials on how to handle the acceptance of non-compliant specialty metal, until a long-term solution could be developed. On June 1, 2006, the Under Secretary of Defense for Acquisition, Technology, and Logistics issued a memorandum which authorized a "conditional acceptance and withholding of payment" based on two considerations: (1) a financial consideration (or offset to the federal government) to support the conditional acceptance, and (2) a comprehensive corrective action plan provided by the contractor.[23]

Congress may want to consider whether to carefully monitor the waiver process to see if the need for waivers has been rendered unnecessary due to recent changes in the law.

Effect on Joint Ventures and Partnerships

There are contrasting views on the effect of the specialty metal clause on joint ventures and partnerships. One view was expressed by some companies that signaled their inability to meet the specialty metal requirement. They were part of the Berry Amendment Reform Coalition, an organization of industry associations that represents thousands of companies that provide products, services, and personnel to the federal government. The coalition asserted that the specialty metal clause could have a harmful effect on the ability of defense contractors to partner with other companies. Prime contractors who relied on small and mid-size companies to deliver components, such as fasteners and components from electronic circuit boards, found compliance with the Berry Amendment difficult. According to the coalition, due to Berry Amendment requirements, the cost of a fastener for a military plane can be as much as five times more than the cost of a fastener for a commercial airplane. Additionally, the cost of using domestic titanium (for a U.S. company) could be as much as 40% higher than the cost of using non-domestic titanium.[24]

Another view was expressed in a 2009 report prepared by the RAND Project Air Force (PAF),[25] which studied factors that affected price fluctuations in titanium. The report concluded that there are a number of market forces and price drivers that affect the domestic titanium industry.[26]

---

[22] http://www.dcma.mil/dnad/. DOD has issued DNADs for a number of items. In the Fastener DNAD, it was determined that satisfactory quality and sufficient quantity of specialty metal in the form of fasteners could not be procured as and when needed. Subsection (b) of 10 U.S.C. 2533b states that if such a determination is made, subsection (a) does not apply. Thus, the restriction in subsection (a) of 10 U.S.C. 2533b does not apply to fasteners. Contracting officers may procure end items, and components thereof, containing fasteners, notwithstanding the country where the specialty metals contained in such items were melted or produced. DOD will revisit the basis for this DNAD if it learns that the circumstances which formed the basis of the determination have changed. Thus, the DNAD will be revised if and when compliant specialty metal of satisfactory quality and sufficient quantity, in the required form, can be procured as and when needed.

[23] Defense Contract Management Agency, Interim Instruction, Non-compliance with the Preference for Domestic Specialty Metals Provision, DFARS 252.225-7014, revised March 10, 2006, 4 p.; and OUSD(A&TL). Memorandum on Berry Amendment Compliance for Specialty Metals, by Kenneth J. Krieg, June 1, 2006, 2 p.

[24] Senate Berry Amendment Streamlining Proposal: Myth versus Reality. A position paper of the Berry Amendment Reform Coalition. July 18, 2006, 4 p. The Berry Amendment Reform Coalition is an organization of about a dozen industry associations that reportedly support alternative approaches that promote a reasonable and balanced solution. http://www.nedassoc.org/.

[25] PAF is a division of the Rand Corporation and the U.S. Air Force's federally funded center for research and analysis. (continued...)

The Administrative Burden

The cost of compliance with administrative requirements of the specialty metal clause could be unsustainable. Many companies report that they are unable to develop a compliance measure that would support a 100% across the board systematic reporting system of every type of metal that is used in the melting process. Such a system of compliance would be difficult, if not impossible, to maintain. Further, since most contractors have smaller percentages of their business line devoted to DOD contracts, it may not be cost-effective for contractors to develop such a system. Many have signaled that if forced to do so, they would terminate their business relationship with DOD and increase their capacity for commercial work.

Congress may want to determine whether the recent amendments to the specialty metals law have substantially mitigated any possible administrative burdens.

Reliability

In Urgent Situations and Times of War

The issue of reliability has been the cornerstone of why domestic source restrictions, like the specialty metal clause, are viewed by some proponents as essential to the viability of the domestic defense industrial base. Central to the issue of reliability is the basic premise upon which the Berry Amendment was first adopted. The Berry Amendment, which dates from the eve of World War II, was established for a narrowly defined purpose: to ensure that U.S. troops wore military uniforms wholly produced within the United States and to ensure that U.S. troops were fed with food products solely produced in the United States.[27] There were at least two congressional concerns: (1) that the United States maintain a vibrant domestic industrial base by requiring that military troops wear uniforms made in the United States, and consume food produced in the United States; and (2) that the nation be prepared in the event of adversity or war.

Many view domestic source restrictions like the specialty metal clause as a way to insure that, in urgent situations and times of war, the United States will have access to critical items needed to ensure national security. Those who advocate for maintaining a robust capability among the domestic sources for titanium, as an example, argue that these companies will ensure that, should a global shortage of titanium develop or if the United States loses a key trading partner, the United States will not become unduly dependent on another country for a critical item. Furthermore, having domestic suppliers who have the protection of the specialty metal clause may ensure that domestic production lines remaining open and viable.

(...continued)

See http://www.rand.org/paf.

[26] Seong, Somi, et al. Titanium: Industrial Base, Price Trends, and Technology Initiatives. *RAND Project AIR FORCE*, March 29, 2009.

[27] On April 5, 1941, the Berry Amendment was enacted as part of the Fiscal Year (FY) 1941 Fifth Supplemental National Defense Appropriations Act, P.L. 77-29, 10 U.S.C. § 2241 note. The Berry Amendment was made permanent when P.L. 102-396, §9005, was amended by P.L. 103-139, §8005. Since then, Congress has regularly added or subtracted Berry Amendment provisions. On December 13, 2001, passage of the FY2002 National Defense Authorization Act codified the Berry Amendment, repealing §§9005 and 8109 of the above-mentioned bills. The Berry Amendment is now codified at 10 U.S.C. 2533a.

Maintaining a Productive and Profitable Domestic Base

An argument that is often raised is that, as an example, the three domestic titanium producers would not be viable if the specialty metal clause did not exist. A look at the three domestic titanium producers reveals that they have different income streams, and are not wholly dependent on the specialty metals clause.

Domestic Restrictions Protect the U.S. Industrial Base

Some policymakers believe that products consumed by Americans should be made at home, and that domestic source provisions like the specialty metal clause represent jobs for the smaller, domestic companies in America. However, when compared to the jobs generated by the major defense contractors in the global supply chain, the number of local jobs is proportionately smaller.

Options for Congress

It is important to note that the specialty metal clause in the Berry Amendment had been in place for over three decades. Any change in the law could likely have both upstream and downstream effects in the defense supply chain. How will the change affect prime contractors and subcontractors on the second, third, and fourth tiers, as well as domestic suppliers?

At least seven possible options for policymakers to consider are listed below: (1) eliminate the specialty metal clause; (2) require an assessment of compliance with new exceptions to the specialty metals clause; (3) require a review of waivers issued under the revised specialty metals clause, including requiring DOD to publicly disclose when waivers are granted; (4) require congressional approval before non-compliant specialty metal can be used in certain defense contracts; (5) require a congressional report for each platform/component where non-compliant specialty metals are used in defense contracts; (6) encourage the use of domestic specialty metal; and (7) appoint a special metals protection board.

Eliminate the Specialty Metal Clause

Congress could eliminate the specialty metal clause as well as the Berry Amendment. Some question whether the Berry Amendment is still a good policy, given the global supply chain; others question whether each item needs the protection of a domestic source policy. Possibly the elimination of the specialty metal clause or the Berry Amendment would be met with fierce opposition, particularly from domestic suppliers without a strong foreign market. To some extent, domestic source restrictions like the Berry Amendment may help to insure that there is a dedicated domestic source for DOD products.

Require an Assessment of Compliance with New Exceptions to the Specialty Metal Clause

Congress could require a comprehensive review of compliance and implementation of the revisions to the new specialty metal clause. Congress could require that GAO complete a study of the frequency and impact of the waiver process, use of exceptions (such as the exceptions for national security, de minimis, and COTS) and evaluate DOD's role in exercising oversight of the implementation of the new provisions.

Require a Review of Waivers Issued Under the Revised Specialty Metal Clause, and for Public Disclosure When Waivers Are Granted

Congress could require a review and publication of the numbers and types of waivers granted (Determinations of Domestic Non-Availability [DNAD])[28] to purchase items that are non-compliant, and tighten the waiver process so that waivers are not granted for inappropriate or arbitrary reasons. Congress could direct DOD to work more closely with the Defense Contract Management Agency to determine if there is greater compliance with the specialty metal clause. On the one hand, requiring more transparency and openness in the waiver process may pose more of an administrative burden on DOD. On the other hand, more transparency may engender more public confidence in the process.

Require Congressional Approval before Non-Compliant Specialty Metal Can Be Used In Defense Contracts

Congress could limit the use of non-compliant specialty metal. One approach is the application of a market-based standard—so that DOD can tie the amount of non-compliant specialty metal permitted to the percentage of business that the contractor has with DOD—so if a contractor acquires 16% of the DOD market, it will be permitted to use compliant specialty metal for at least 16% of its total market needs.

As an example set forth in 10 U.S.C. 2306(b), Congress enacted six legal criteria that must be met for the Multi-Year Procurement Program (MYP) to be operational, and has reached conclusions as to when a weapons program does not meet all of the requirements for MVP.[29] The process has been perceived, for the most part, as fair and balanced.

Such a set of conditions could determine under what circumstances non-compliant specialty metal could be used in defense contracts, and might include the following criteria:

- That the use of non-compliant specialty metal will result in a substantial savings of the total anticipated costs throughout the life of the contract;
- That the percentage of specialty metal used for the weapons program is expected to remain substantially unchanged during the contract period, in terms of rate of production and procurement, and total quantities;
- That the contract for the use of non-compliant specialty metal will be subject to re-competition on a five-year basis, to give the domestic specialty metal industry an opportunity to develop the capacity and capability to meet future program requirements;
- That the estimates of both the cost of the contract and the anticipated cost avoidance are realistic and supportable through independent audits and investigations;

---

[28] http://www.acq.osd.mil/dpap/cpic/ic/domestic_non-availability_determinations_dnads.html.

[29] According to the Defense Acquisition University, a multi-year procurement (MYP) is "a method of competitively purchasing up to 5 years' requirements in one contract, funded annually as appropriations permit." Congress set up specific rules that must be met before a program gains MYP status.

- That there is a reasonable expectation that throughout the life of the contemplated contract period, the head of the military service will request funding for the contract, at the level required, to avoid contract cancellation; and
- That the use of such non-compliant specialty metal, in this particular weapons system, is critical to the national security of the United States.

Require a Congressional Report for Each Platform/Component Where Foreign Specialty Metals are used in Defense Contracts

One approach that Congress may consider is to require DOD to produce a separate report for each platform or component of a weapons program where foreign specialty metals are used. For example, in the Future Combat System, where there are about 20-24 separate platforms, each platform would be supported by a separate report which calculates the sources, types, and percentages of specialty metal content, both foreign and domestic.

Examining the specialty metal content by platform may uncover data that are often buried in the aggregate numbers of larger reports on the entire weapons program. The level and specificity of detail could pose an administrative burden on DOD and defense contractors.

Encourage the Use of Domestic Specialty Metal

Congress could develop steps to further support a stronger domestic specialty metal industry. One alternative is to encourage the development of technological capabilities and advances by providing tax incentives for investment in scientific and manufacturing technology. Congress could create a socioeconomic subsidy program to support the domestic specialty metal suppliers; one approach would be to create a partnership between DOD and domestic suppliers. Such an approach was described as a way to develop a greater capacity to meet the delivery requirements for aviation parts in the military, as noted in the FY2007 National Defense Appropriations Act, P.L. 109-289, where the increased demand for domestic steel suppliers was highlighted:

> The Department of Defense's demand for iron-based alloy aviation specialty steels has dramatically increased as a result of continuing deployments to the overseas theaters of operation. Today, there is only one domestic supplier for a unique process which utilizes vacuum inducted melt/vacuum arc re-melt, the process which gives aviation grade steels their required properties. These specialty steels are critical to building high technology U.S. military weapon systems. Further, there has been a related and dramatic increase in the raw material needed to make these specialty steels. Lead times for these raw materials have grown from 3 months to 1 year. According to the Army, the overall effect on lead times for spare part deliverables has swelled in some cases to greater than 24 months. As such, the conferees encourage the Department of Defense to partner with domestic industry to develop a greater capacity to meet the delivery requirements for aviation parts to the military within an acceptable time frame. The conferees suggest that the Department explore a 50/50 cost share project between the Federal government, private industry, and state governments as the best means to create this capacity as rapidly as possible.[30]

---

[30] H.Rept. 109-676.

Appoint a New Specialty Metals Protection Board

The House of Representatives has expressed concern over the conclusions expressed by the Specialty Metals Protection Board, particularly over the Board's definition of what constitutes a critical and strategic material. In the House Armed Services Committee report accompanying both the FY2009 and FY2010 National Defense Authorization Acts, it was noted that the conclusions reached by the Board were unacceptable. Excerpts from the House report accompanying H.R. 2647, the FY2010 National Defense Authorization Act, appear below.[31]

> This definition limits the purview of the Board to only those materials for which the determinations the Board is tasked to make are presupposed in the definition of the materials themselves. Furthermore, such a definition fails to include a range of materials that Congress has designated as critical to national security and, as such, has provided significant protection or domestic preference in DOD policy and in statute. For example, Congress has determined that reliance on foreign sources of supply for materials such as titanium, specialty steel, and high performance magnets, poses a heightened risk. The Board's narrowing of the definition of materials critical to national security renders the Board unable to provide perspective on the adequacy, suitability, or effectiveness of those policies. Moreover, it limits the ability of the Board to consider any course of action, however minor, in relation to a material until the point at which potential damage to national security is imminent and severe. It also creates the perverse situation that a material could be critical to every element of the industrial base upon which the Department depends, but not considered critical to the Department itself if the material is also used significantly in commercial items. As an indication of the inadequacy of this definition for the Board's functioning, the Board currently identifies only one material as meeting the definition for consideration as a strategic material critical to national security. The committee does not find this conclusion to be plausible and expects that the Board will swiftly revisit this definition to ensure that it is able to identify gaps in our domestic defense supply chain and provide the President, the Secretary of Defense, and Congress with information, analysis, and advice on strategic materials which are critical to the operations of the Department of Defense.

Congress could follow the example of the Packard Commission by creating an independent body to study the specialty metal clause and its impact on the defense industry.[32] By requiring an independent review chartered by Congress, industry experts could be consulted to determine if DOD's determination that only one material is "critical" to national security and that specialty metals do not require domestic preference are reasonable.

Legislation

Legislation passed in the 112th Congress

H.R. 4310, the National Defense Authorization Act for FY2013, contains a provision which broaden the definition of specialty metals produced within the United States. Section 817 would

---

[31] U.S. Congress, House Armed Services Committee, H.Rept. 111-166, *Report on H.R. 2647: National Defense Authorization Act for Fiscal Year 2010*, P.L. 111-84, signed into law on October 28, 2009.

[32] In July 1985, President Reagan asked David Packard, chairman of the Hewlett-Packard Corporation and a former Deputy Secretary of Defense, to chair an independent Blue Ribbon Commission which came to be known as the Packard Commission. The Packard Commission was directed to conduct a broad study of defense management including the budget process, procurement, organization and operation, and legislative oversight, and to make recommendations for streamlining and improving defense management. Executive Order 12526, July 15, 1986.

amend 10 U.S.C. 2533b to include "melted, or processed in a manner that results in physical or chemical property changes that are the equivalent of melting." The term "produced" does not include finishing processes such as "rolling, heat treatment, quenching, tempering, grinding, or shaving."[33]

H.R. 4310 also contains a provision, Section 901, which reconfigures the membership and scope of the Strategic Materials Protection Board (SMPB) by requiring that the Deputy Assistant Secretary of Defense for Manufacturing and Industrial Base Policy serve as chair. The congressional intent of such a restructuring can be found in a statement of findings that accompanies the bill. Excerpts from the bill follow.

TITLE IX—DEPARTMENT OF DEFENSE ORGANIZATION AND MANAGEMENT

Subtitle A—Department of Defense Management

SEC. 901. ADDITIONAL DUTIES OF DEPUTY ASSISTANT SECRETARY OF DEFENSE FOR MANUFACTURING AND INDUSTRIAL BASE POLICY AND AMENDMENTS TO STRATEGIC MATERIALS PROTECTION BOARD.

(a) Findings- Congress finds the following:

(1) The Defense Logistics Agency has made little progress in addressing the findings and recommendations from the April 2009 report of the Department of Defense report titled 'Reconfiguration of the National Defense Stockpile Report to Congress'.

(2) The office of the Deputy Assistant Secretary of Defense for Manufacturing and Industrial Base Policy has historically analyzed the United States defense industrial base from the point of view of prime contractors and original equipment manufacturers and has provided insufficient attention to producers of materials critical to national security, including raw materials producers.

(3) Responsibility for the secure supply of materials critical to national security, which supports the defense industrial base, is decentralized throughout the Department of Defense.

(4) The office of the Deputy Assistant Secretary of Defense for Manufacturing and Industrial Base Policy should expand its focus to consider both a top-down view of the supply chain, beginning with prime contractors, and a bottom-up view that begins with raw materials suppliers.

(5) To enable this focus and support a more coherent, comprehensive strategy as it pertains to materials critical to national security, the office of the Deputy Assistant Secretary of Defense for Manufacturing and Industrial Base Policy should develop policy, conduct oversight, and monitor resource allocation for agencies of the Department of Defense, including the Defense Logistics Agency, for all activities that pertain to ensuring a secure supply of materials critical to national security.

(6) The Strategic Materials Protection Board should be reconfigured so as to be chaired by the Deputy Assistant Secretary of Defense for Manufacturing and Industrial Base Policy and should fully execute its duties and responsibilities.[34]

---

[33] H.R. 4310 was introduced on March 29, 2012, passed on a recorded vote on May 12, 2013, and referred to the Senate Armed Sources Committee on July 19, 2912.

[34] H.R. 4310, Title 9, Department of Defense Organization and Management, Subtitle A, Department of Defense Management.

H.R. 3449, Defense Supply Chain and Industrial Base Security Act was introduced on November 16, 2011, and referred to the House Armed Services Committee. The bill would require the Secretary of Defense to

> (1) develop a defense supply chain and industrial base strategy, and subsequent plan, designed to secure the supply chain and industrial base sectors determined to be critical to U.S. national security;
>
> (2) review the strategy and plan on a biennial basis; and
>
> (3) report to Congress on the strategy and plan, as well as on the results of each review.[35]

FY2008 National Defense Authorization Act and Revisions to Existing Specialty Metal Rules

P.L. 110-181, the FY2008 National Defense Authorization Act, contained three new provisions which affect the specialty metal clause:

- Section 803 required the Strategic Materials Protection Board to perform an assessment of the viability of domestic producers of strategic materials, the purpose of which is to assess which domestic producers are investing, or plan to invest on a sustained basis, in the development of a continued domestic production capability of strategic materials to meet national defense requirements. Such an assessment would be evaluated and weighted in any decision to grant future waivers to the specialty metal clause.[36]

Sections 804 and 884 included these provisions:

- Applies to contracts or subcontracts for the acquisition of specialty metals, including mill products, such as bar, billet, slab, wire, plate and sheet, that have not been incorporated into end items, subsystems, assemblies, or components;
- Applies to contracts or subcontracts for the acquisition of forgings or castings of specialty metals, unless such forgings or castings are incorporated into commercially available off-the-shelf end items, subsystems, or assemblies;
- Applies to contracts or subcontracts for commercially available, high performance magnets unless such high performance magnets are incorporated into commercially available, off-the-shelf-end items or subsystems;
- Applies to contracts or subcontracts for commercially available off-the-shelf fasteners (some exceptions noted);
- Applies to contracts for electronic components unless the Secretary of Defense, upon the recommendation of the Strategic Materials Protection Board pursuant to Section 187 of this title, determines that the domestic availability of a particular electronic component is critical to national security;
- Provides exceptions for the Secretary of Defense or the Secretary of a military department to accept delivery of an item containing specialty metals that were not melted in the United States, if the total amount of noncompliant specialty

---

[35] H.R. 3449, Bill Summary, Legislative Information Service.

[36] §803. Reinvestment in Domestic Sources of Strategic Materials, P.L. 110-181.

metals in the item does not exceed 2% of the total weight of specialty metals in the item (excludes high performance magnets);

- Provides exceptions for the Secretary of Defense or the Secretary of a military department to acquire commercial derivative military articles, under certain conditions; and
- Provides waivers for national security if the Secretary of Defense determines in writing that acceptance of such end items is necessary to the national security interests of the United States, under certain conditions.

FY2007 National Defense Authorization Act and the Enactment of a New Specialty Metal Clause

Congress enacted provisions in the FY2007 National Defense Authorization Act that changed the statutory authority for the special metal clause. P.L. 109-364 created a new specialty metal clause separate from the Berry Amendment, moving it into a separate section of Title 10.[37] Also, Section 842b established a one-time waiver of the Berry Amendment for non-compliant specialty metal incorporated into items produced, manufactured, or assembled in the United States before the date of the act's enactment. DOD can grant waivers provided the noncompliance was not knowing or willful.[38]

Section 842 of the FY2007 National Defense Authorization Act

- Creates a new section, 10 U.S.C. 2533b, in the U.S. Code;
- Reaffirms that any specialty metal (e.g., raw stock) acquired directly by the government or by a prime contractor for delivery to the government, must be melted or produced in the United States. This restriction applies to all tiers of subcontractors when acquiring aircraft, missile and space systems, ships, tank and automotive items, weapons systems, or ammunition;
- Restricts not only the procurement of the specialty metal in these items, but restricts procurement of the end items, and components thereof, that contain specialty metals;
- Prohibits the practice of withholding contract payment while conditionally accepting noncompliant items in these categories;
- Provides a national security exemption, where the Secretary of Defense or the Secretary of the military service can waive the specialty metal compliance requirement when compliant specialty metal, of a satisfactory quality, quantity, and in the required form cannot be procured as needed and when needed;
- Exempts procurement outside the United States in support of combat or contingency operation;
- Exempts sole source procurements based on unusual and compelling urgency of need;

---

[37] 10 U.S.C. 2533b.
[38] FARS 225.7003-4.

- Provides exceptions for procurements related to international agreements (e.g., qualifying countries), non-appropriated fund contracts, and small purchases (i.e., less than the simplified acquisition threshold); and
- Provides for a "de minimis" exception which means that up to 2% of non-compliant specialty metal can be included in electronic components.[39]

Strategic Materials Protection Board

Section 843 of FY2007 National Defense Authorization Act required the creation of a Strategic Materials Protection Board to determine which items should be designated as critical to national security, and to recommend changes for future domestic sourcing.

2007 Meeting of the Strategic Materials Protection Board

The board held its first meeting on July 17, 2007, and reached the following conclusions as described here:

- the term "materials critical to national security" would be taken to mean "strategic materials critical to national security" or simply "strategic materials," and would include those specialty metals listed in 10 U.S.C. 2533b, and any other materials that the board chose to so designate;
- the board's efforts would initially focus on determining the need to take action to ensure a long-term domestic supply of specialty metals as designated in 10 U.S.C. 2533b;
- the board adopted certain Terms of Reference to shape its deliberations; and
- the board directed its executive secretary to conduct an initial analysis of national security issues associated with strategic materials, and to report the results of that analysis at the next SMPB meeting.[40]

2008 Meeting of the Strategic Material Protection Board

The board held its second meeting on December 12, 2008, and reached the following conclusions as described here:

- Approved a definition of "strategic material" and "critical material" proposed by the executive secretary were discussed and approved by the board;
- Reviewed and validated the work of the Strategic and Critical Materials Working Group in response to congressionally directed requirements of H.Rept. 109-89 and S.Rept. 110-55;
- Validated an "Initial Analysis of National Security Issues Associated with Strategic Materials" and authorized its publication in the Federal Register; and

---

[39] The final rule was published in the Federal Register (FR Doc No: E9-17967, Federal Register, Volume 74, Issue 144, Wednesday, July 29, 2009.) The final rule under DFARS Case 2008–D003 defined "produce" to mean "the application of forces or processes to a specialty metal to create the desired physical properties through quenching or tempering of steel plate, gas atomization or sputtering of titanium, or final consolidation of non-melt derived titanium powder or titanium alloy powder." http://www.gpo.gov/fdsys/pkg/FR-2009-07-29/html/E9-17967.htm.

[40] Office of the Under Secretary of Defense (Acquisition, Technology & Logistics.) First meeting of the Strategic Materials Protection Board, September 2007, p. 2.

- Revised the Terms of Reference to reflect their new definitions for strategic and critical materials, providing the board with more flexibility to examining future issues, and broadening their scope to address additional matters associated with strategic materials.[41]

Based on the recommendations of the December 2008 meeting of the Strategic Materials Protection Board, DOD has determined that specialty metals no longer require domestic source protection, as described below in excerpts from the report to Congress.

> The key finding of this analysis is that specialty metals, as defined in 10 U.S.C. 2533b, are not "materials critical to national security" for which only a U.S. source should be used; and there is no national security reason for the Department to take action to ensure a long term domestic supply of these specialty metals. The "criticality" of a material is a function of its importance in DOD applications, the extent to which DOD actions are required to shape and sustain the market, and the impact and likelihood of supply disruption. The analysis showed that specialty metals are "strategic materials" which may require special monitoring and attention/action; but not, in general, a domestic source restriction. Should reliable supplies/capacities be insufficient to meet potential requirements for a projected conflict, other risk mitigation options, including stockpiling, could represent an effective alternative.

> High purity beryllium, however, is a critical material. Even in peacetime, defense applications dominate the market; it is essential for important defense systems and unique in the function it performs. In addition, domestic production capabilities have atrophied, and there are no reliable foreign suppliers. Accordingly, the Department should continue to take those special actions necessary to maintain a long term domestic supply of high purity beryllium. In fact, the Department has established a Title III of the Defense Production Act project with U.S. supplier Brush-Wellman to build and operate a new high purity beryllium production facility.

> The Strategic Materials Protection Board (SMPB) should review and validate any internal or external recommendations that identify strategic materials that are essential for a wide variety of important defense applications and for which there is a relatively high potential for supply disruption. For example, a relatively high potential for supply disruption would be represented by a situation in which reliable supplies (U.S. or non-U.S.) are projected to be insufficient to support the defense needs of the United States during peacetime and/or during a conflict. In such circumstances, DOD market intervention such as increasing or establishing reliable production capability and/or stockpiling may be an effective risk mitigation strategy.[42]

Annual Industrial Capabilities Report to Congress

Title 10 of the United States Code, Section 2504, requires the Secretary of Defense to report to the House and Senate Armed Services Committees on the viability of the defense industrial base including the following information:

---

[41] Office of the Under Secretary of Defense (Acquisition, Technology & Logistics), Deputy Under Secretary of Defense (Industrial Policy), and the Executive Secretary to the Strategic Materials Protection Board. Report of the Meeting of the Department of Defense Strategic Protection Materials Board. December 12, 2008, pages 1-4.

[42] Office of the Under Secretary of Defense (Acquisition, Technology & Logistics), Deputy Under Secretary of Defense (Industrial Policy), and the Executive Secretary to the Strategic Materials Protection Board. Report of the Meeting of the Department of Defense Strategic Materials Board. December 12, 2008, p. 5-6. A summary of the Board's analysis and conclusions were published in the Federal Register, Vol. 74. No. 34, February 23, 2009, pages 8061-8064.

(1) A description of the departmental guidance prepared pursuant to section 2506 of this Title.

(2) A description of the methods and analyses being undertaken by the Department of Defense alone or in cooperation with other Federal agencies, to identify and address concerns regarding technological and industrial capabilities of the national technology and industrial base.

(3) A description of the assessments prepared pursuant to section 2505 of this Title and other analyses used in developing the budget submission of the Department of Defense for the next fiscal year.

(4) Identification of each program designed to sustain specific essential technological and industrial capabilities and processes of the national technology and industrial base."

2012 Report to Congress

The 2012 Annual Industrial Capabilities Report to Congress can be accessed online.[43]

Author Contact Information

Valerie Bailey Grasso
Specialist in Defense Acquisition
vgrasso@crs.loc.gov, 7-7617

---

[43] Department of Defense. Office of Under Secretary of Defense for Acquisition, Technology & Logistics Industrial Policy. Annual Industrial Capabilities Report to Congress, May 2010, at http://www.acq.osd mil/mibp/docs/annual_ind_cap_rpt_to_congress-2012.pdf.

www.ingramcontent.com/pod-product-compliance
Lightning Source LLC
Chambersburg PA
CBHW081822170526
45167CB00008B/3510